GRAFFITI IN THE BIG TEN

Marina N. Haan

Richard B. Hammerstrom

Printed by Brown House Galleries,
P.O. Box 4243, Madison, WI 53711

International Standard Book Number:
0-9604534-0-7

THANKS

The authors extend their thanks to all those who helped pull this off. In particular we thank Kay, Bruce, Barry, Brad and Jody Poltermann of Poltermann Transfers, Inc., Leighton Holtz, and Rich Hayes.

DEDICATION

This book is dedicated to all
custodians who have never removed,
expunged, erased, covered, or other-
wise defaced a piece of graffiti.

CHAPTERS

Authors' Note

We did it for Truth.

> Marina N. Haan
> Richard B. Hammerstrom

Truth flies like an arrow.

Fruit flies like a banana.

> Second stall, men's room
> English Department
> University of Wisconsin

There lies in the heart of the North American continent, in an area generally identified as the Upper Midwest, a series of strange enclaves. These outposts are known individually as campuses, and collectively as the Big Ten. Their inhabitants are called students.

While the scientific community has studied the Big Ten students for sometime, there remain untold mysteries regarding their behavioral patterns. It was in the hope of resolving some of these riddles that we, the authors, initiated our search into the unknown.

Previous Big Ten researchers had gone about their business somewhat distantly. They had made liberal use of observation, surveys, and questionnaires, but had made little or no direct contact with the students.

Well, none of that for us. We were determined to go to the root of the matter. We wanted to know not what the students had recorded for researchers, but what they had recorded for themselves. The only means of determining this was to penetrate the most intimate environment of the students. Thus it was that we initiated a massive gathering of graffiti in the toilets of the Big Ten.

The data accumulated in that Herculean research effort has been analyzed and categorized and is presented in its entirety in the following pages. We trust that the product of our labors will provide significant assistance to behavioral scientists and others in their efforts to unveil the mysteries of the Big Ten student of the 1980's.

Who am us anyway?

Wisconsin-Spudnuts Restaurant

Big Ten graffitiists devote a considerable portion of their talents on their role as students.   There are varied opinions.

We are the people our parents warned us about and the ones we will warn our children about.

Wisconsin-Memorial Library

Human: an erudite ape with less hair and more money.
College Student: a pre-erudite ape with more hair and
less money.

Wisconsin-Memorial Library

Frat boys have no balls. They have to have their parents buy them friends and security.

Ohio State-Thompson Library

Sororities turn great women into stuck-up bitches.

Purdue-Library

School is a WOW!!!

Wisconsin-Memorial Library

School is like that ol' North Wind — it blows!

Iowa-Library

Life is a bitch; school is its son.

Iowa-Library

What time is it? It depends who you ask. The administration always says that it is too early until it is too late.

Wisconsin-North Hall

To err is human; to forgive is against university policy.

Wisconsin-White Library

When I think back on all the crap that I learned in High
School, it's a wonder that I can think at all.

Purdue-Library

PhD - piled high and deep.

Iowa-Engineering

If you can't hack it, then pick up your marbles and go home.

Michigan-Hatcher Library

Quality education? Hah! Hah! Hah!

Michigan-Undergraduate Library

Lemmings! All of you!

Michigan-Undergraduate Library

You exist; it's this place that is unreal.

Purdue-Library

I had better make a lot of money when I get out of this
learning institution.

Purdue-Library

If you think education is expensive, try ignorance.

Ohio State-Thompson Library

So if the cards are played right today, we could be looking forward to a brighter future.

Michigan-Hatcher Library

The dumb ass behind me is eating Doritos while I'm trying to study for an exam.

-below-

Well, the dummy behind me is eating an apple.

Ohio State-Thompson Library

Finals cause excessive brain damage.

Iowa-Library

Finals should become an unfair labor practice.

Purdue-Library

I do not love thee, Dr. Fell.

Michigan-Undergraduate Library

Live it, laugh it, or eat it.

Michigan State-Chemistry

Lives are held within these walls.

Iowa-Library

Neuroses are red.
Melancholia is blue.
I'm schizophrenic.
What are you?

Wisconsin-Social Science

Yes, you must leave everything you can't control.
It starts with your family and later gets around to your soul.

Wisconsin-YMCA

If you can't eat it or fuck it, piss on it.

Michigan State-Engineering

Forget the broads.
Forget the booze.
Just don't forget
my hockey news.

Illinois-Lincoln Hall

Keep your mouth shut and let them think you're stupid; no
sense opening it and removing all doubt.

Michigan State-North Kedzie

Lately there has been an alarming increase in things about which I know nothing.

Northwestern-Harris Hall

Just keep telling yourself, "Someday these will be the best years of my life."

Wisconsin-Law

Booze is fine.
Sex is great.
Finally I get to graduate.

Purdue-Library

Too weeks ago I coon't even spell injuneer, and now I are one.

Michigan-Undergraduate Library

Everywhere one finds evidence of the students' commitment to their fields of study.

Do math majors have socks?

Indiana-Swain Hall

Calculus majors have functional deficiencies.

Indiana-Swain Hall

Phuck physics!

Wisconsin-Physics

Physics sucks air at 40 psi.

Ohio State-Smith Laboratory

If you laid the pencil-headed physicists head to head you would form a line 1" wide circling the world twice.

Purdue-Library

Physics professors complain about their pay, but when they do do work they get joules.

Minnesota-Tate Laboratory

Physicists phuck phrogs!

Iowa-Basic Science Building

Physiologists eat hormones!

Wisconsin-Agronomy

Botanists never take a shit, just a P-protein.

Wisconsin-Botany

Why is a chemistry professor's piss yellow and semen white? That's the only way he knows if he's coming or going.

Iowa-Chemistry & Botany

Fuck organic!
>   *-below-*
You mean you can fuck synthetic?
>   *Indiana-Chemistry*

I thought drugs were fun until I started studying pharmacy.
>   *Michigan-Little Science Building*

It is every pharmacist's responsibility to do drugs.
>   *Iowa-Pharmacy*

Proctology is for shit!
>   *Indiana-Myers Hall*

Psychology is disturbing God's natural order.
>   *Minnesota-Elliott Hall*

Psychology psucks!
>   *-below-*
Psame to you!
>   *Minnesota-Elliott Hall*

Most guys find it to piss; engineers piss to find it.
>   *Iowa-Engineering*

Engineers do it with precision.
                    -below-
The last thing you need is precision.

                              Iowa-Engineering

If it weren't for engineers the manufacturers of white
socks would be out of business.

                    Michigan-West Engineering

Let's be aerotic!
                    -below-
Or aeronautie!

                    Minnesota-Aeronautic Eng.

Chemical engineers suck heat pumps!

                    Michigan-West Engineering

Ode to thermodynamics:
Here I sit and never cycled,
tried to shit but only mikol'ed.

                Wisconsin-Chemical Engineering

McArthur was wrong — Law School is Hell.

                    Wisconsin-Law

"We'll kill the lawyers first." Shakespeare, King Hernry V. Isn't it time?

Wisconsin-English

Don't read History; make it.

Michigan State-Engineering

If you are a History major, this is the only job you'll ever have.

Wisconsin-History

Learn from the past; don't take History.

Wisconsin-History

Political Science is a joke.

Illinois-Lincoln Hall

The study of Economics is:
> *-below-*

-reality constrained to a worthless abstract model
> *-below-*

-a method of legitimizing the social status quo
> *-below-*

-never having to say you're sorry
> *-below-*

-bucks, fucks and a lot of yuks.

Wisconsin-Economics

Why do we study poverty instead of wealth?

Wisconsin-Economics

Neo-classical economics kills intellectualism.

Wisconsin-Economics

You can be a business major and be cool, but there aren't too many of us.

Iowa-Phillips Hall

I'm a grad and I'm not too bright,
but I major in Business and I do alright.
I never study, but I get B's,
and I'm always ready to drop to my knees.
The reason for this is not to pray,
but to grab my prof and suck away.
I may be dumb, but I learn quick —
to get ahead in Business, you have to suck dick!

Iowa-Phillips Hall

Business student: Are you taking psychology?
Psychology student: Why do you ask?

Minnesota-Elliott Hall

We come to the holocaust of business potentials.

Iowa-Phillips Hall

Most people in business must soon be dealt with.

Michigan-Hatcher Library

Hells! Bells! Accounting smells!

Purdue-Library

I got into accounting!
            -below-
Congratulations! I got into clap.

Michigan State-Giltner Hall

Who is this Phil Osophy, and why is he tormenting me?

Wisconsin-Philosophy

Old Plato saw both mind and matter.
Thomas Hobbes saw but the latter.
Now poor Thom's soul doth rot in Hell.
Quoth God, "It's immaterial."

Wisconsin-Philosophy

Philosophy majors have no sense of meter.

Indiana-Sycamore Hall

Epistemology is only one aspect of ontology.

Iowa-Gilmore Hall

Linguistics is the exact opposite of screaming.

Iowa-Lindley Hall

It isn't Art until it hurts.

Wisconsin-Humanities

Art for Art's sake!

-below-

Money for God's sake!

Michigan-Undergraduate Library

Art is beauty!

-below-

-my deceased grandfather

-below-

-a window-washer on State Street

-below-

-an anagram for tar.

Wisconsin-Humanities

Craft is creation!

-below-

-a cheese factory

-below-

-the punk who broke my finger in ninth grade.

Wisconsin-Humanities

Art is too long!   Life is too short!

Iowa-Art

Art Zinnarut.

Wisconsin-Humanities

Music is the greatness that fills the soul.

Michigan State-Library

Dance, dance, dance
into my pants, pants, pants.

Wisconsin-Lathrop Hall

Afraid of that great big world out there?   Then why not
become a ROTC lifer.

Ohio State-Thompson Library

I love this fucking
university, and this
university loves fucking me.

Michigan-Business

The alma mater is often warmly recalled.

If the doctor gives you a year to live, spend it at I.U.
and it will seem like an eternity.

Indiana-Lindley Hall

If God gave the world an enema, I.U. would get the tube.

Indiana-Morrison Hall

Swain Hall is the 8th wonder of the world; it's the only hole above ground.

Indiana-Swain Hall

Goodbye I.U.! You served your artificial purpose.

Indiana-Rawles Hall

Who's your woman?
Hoosier woman!!!

Indiana-Swain Hall

Proceed large Crimson!

Indiana-Swain Hall

Roses are red.
Violets are blue.
Catch snatch at I.U.
and V.D. at Purdue.

Purdue-Library

Purdue — where men are men and women are too.

Purdue-Library

Here? At Purdon't?

Purdue-Library

National Limp Dick Award - Purdue University for the greatest number of sexually frustrated men.

Purdue-Library

God created the world in six days, but it took him four years to graduate from Purdue.

Purdue-Library

This place sucks!!!
>   *-below-*

Parental attitude check: My mother says this place sucks, too.
>   *-below-*

Religious attitude check: My minister says this place sucks, too.
>   *-below-*

Airforce attitude check: I hear there's a place down there that sucks.
>   *-below-*

Army attitude check: The other side of this swamp sucks.
>   *-below-*

Marine attitude check: I like it here!

Purdue-Library

Dare to be great — transfer.

Iowa-Engineering

All in all, Michigan sucks!

Michigan-Hatcher Library

No one is a virgin at Michigan, this school fucks everybody!

Michigan-East Engineering

U of M is like a prostitute — you pay to get fucked.

Michigan-Union

U of M is a profit orgy.

Michigan-Union

Keep Michigan beautiful — throw your garbage in Ohio.

Michigan State-Agriculture

This is still Woody's university.

-below-

But does he want it?

Ohio State-Thompson Library

Woody, Woody, Woody, we hated to see you go. (tee hee)

Michigan-Undergraduate Library

Woody is a pecker.

Michigan State-Agriculture

U of Michigan, get Lovelace at quarterback — she doesn't choke on the big ones.

Michigan State-Physics

MSU sucks!

Michigan-Hatcher Library

Michigan sucks footballs!

Ohio State-Thompson Library

Watch out for Illinois women, they eat your sausage and smoke your cigarettes.

-below-

I've only met one, but she smoked my sausage and ate my cigarettes.

Indiana-Lindley Hall

Where the hell is Terre Haute?

Purdue-Library

Graffiti is for people who can't write books.

Wisconsin-Social Science

Big Ten graffitiists may not write books, but they write volumes on their favorite pastime.

Graffiti is beauty and creativity.

Wisconsin-Psychology

This entire wall should be on display at Hopkins Gallery; it's the best piece of art done in this building in many years.

Ohio State-Hopkins Hall

This wall will soon appear as a Bantam Paperback.

Minnesota-Murphy Hall

Restaurants with good graffiti are at the pinnacle of eatery.

Wisconsin-Spudnuts Restaurant

This wall is in its 14th Edition.

Illinois-Lincoln Hall

Support people's art; write on your local bathroom walls.

Wisconsin-Spudnuts Restaurant

Coming soon! Campus-wide graffiti judging contest! Get your entries in early! Winning entries receive:
1. A felt tip pen of your choice.
2. Free 30 minute consultation with three burly custodians.
3. Free transportation to six campus area toilet stalls.

Wisconsin-425 Henry Mall

It appears that creativity has taken a vacation.

Ohio State-Hafferty Hall

Who said the great poets of tomorrow aren't already dead?

Wisconsin-Chemical Engineering

Graffiti is the poetry of the simple-minded.

Purdue-Library

I'm so happy to be able to read this display of intelligence I could just shit.

Iowa-Phillips Hall

The dimensions of the various and sundry rubric previously discussed are by and large intangible.

Wisconsin-425 Henry Mall

Just reading this stuff is getting me fucked up.

Indiana-Chemistry

Whatever happened to the nice men with a little more self-pride and reservation?

-below-

By reading the shit on this desk I would say the fuckers are an endangered species.

Ohio State-Library

Obscenity is the crutch of inarticulate fuckers.

Michigan-Business

Why do so many sickies write graffiti instead of going to shrinks?

-below-

Writing graffiti doesn't cost $40.00 per hour.

Ohio State-Library

Big Ten graffitiists are not inhibited by lack of words.

Couldn't think of anything to write, so I just drew this fuckin' flower.

Wisconsin-Social Science

(graph + feetie)
Indiana-Swain Hall

Sometimes graffiti lasts forever and ever . . .

Go eat a rutabaga!
        -below-
By golly, I wrote this little piece of graffiti when I was just a freshman here at OSU, and now I am a graduating senior, and it's still here. What a mark to leave on an institution of higher learning.

Ohio State-Thompson Library

. . . but sometimes it doesn't.

Who erased my termpaper?

Michigan-Business

Always there is the battle between the student graffitiist and the purveyors of decency and tidiness.

The painter's job was all in vain,
the shithouse poet strikes again.

Classic on all campuses

May the painter of this wall suffer terminal impotence.

Michigan State-Natural Science

Just think, some poor bastard worked all last summer to get this graffiti off here.
-below-
We'll have to make sure he has a job next summer.
-below-
Here's to you, you poor bastard.
-below-
This is called "job security". Signed: The Poor Bastard.

Purdue-Main Library

They wash these walls to suppress my lore,
but the bathroom bohemian has struck once more.

Ohio State-Thompson Library

Janitor, you erased Truth.

Michigan-Education

The truth is, everyone is a connoisseur of graffiti.

Will all you freshies stop writing on the compartment.
                    -below-
The what? I thought this was a fuckin' toilet.

Ohio State-Thompson Library

Do females write stupid horny graffiti too?

Michigan-Graduate Library

Bathroom walls are like nothing so much as cereal boxes;
one reads them while engaged in an unrelated solitary activity.

Minnesota-Zoology

Despite the fact that some people simply communicate better
with their pants down, stall choosing is an art to the graffiti
freak.

Wisconsin-Social Science

(below crude drawing of a penis) The original hangs in the
Whitney Museum. This is a poor reproduction.

Wisconsin-Humanities

Graffiti may be funny but it won't get you tenure.

Wisconsin-Memorial Library

If people were as wise as graffiti is plentiful, then who knows how much better life would be.

Purdue-Main Library

Ulysses contains, in code, all of the graffiti written on the walls of Dublin.

Illinois-Murphy's Bar

Graffiti won't solve war.
            -below-
        -or poverty
            -below-
        -or over-population
            -below-
        -or starvation
            -below-
        -or polution
            -below-
        -or spelling.

Wisconsin-Commerce

You too can write on walls.
            -below-
Sometimes it is enough to drink my tea and put my words on paper.

Wisconsin-Humanities

Is there something about lesbians that makes people want
to write on john walls?
>>>>>> *-below-*
Digital dexterity.

Indiana-Memorial Union

Where is all that wry repartee' that is supposed to be on
this wall?
>>>>>> *-below-*
Wry repartee' is on leave this semester.

Wisconsin-North Hall

Roses are red.
Violets are blue.
God in Heaven
knows I love you.
But the Devil will get us all
for writing on the wall.

Indiana-Memorial Union

If you're reading this you're at a 60° angle.

(at bottom of stall door)

Indiana-Memorial Union

The creativity of the Big Ten graffitiist is often fired by the objects in his immediate vicinity. A favored stimulus is the familiar toilet paper dispenser. This apparatus is frequently labeled by a scrawled arrow leading from a piece of graffiti such as the following.

Nixon tapes — seize one.

Michigan State-Engineering

Do not rotate over 3,600 rpm.

Minnesota-Aeronautic Eng.

U.S. Dollar

Michigan-Undergrad Library

Another fine abrasive by 3M.

Wisconsin-Law

University of Michigan diplomas.

Michigan State-Chemistry

Free typing paper.

Indiana-Swain Hall

The job isn't finished until the paperwork is done.

Minnesota-Vicent Hall

Wipe away your sin.

Michigan-Mason Hall

Millions for defense; not $1 for decent paper.

Michigan State-Chemistry

New York City bonds.

Iowa-Phillips

Northwestern Commemorative Plaques

Northwestern-Education

Monochromatic litmus paper.

Minnesota-Smith Chemistry

(over adjacent dispensers)
Regular . . . . . Unleaded

Michigan State-Engineering

Signs, too, become targets of student playfulness.

(under "No Smoking" sign)
Violators will be violated!

Michigan-Graduate Library

(under "Keep Door Closed" sign)
When passing through.

Northwestern-Kresge Hall

(under "No Entry" sign)
The boogey man lives inside.

Michigan-Graduate Library

Actually, it appears that Big Ten graffitiists will respond to just about any stimulus.

(hole in wall) Sperm bank night depository.

Minnesota-Kolthoff Hall

(squashed mosquito on wall) This is what drunk flying will get you.

Purdue-Main Library

(arrow to bottom of stall door) Beware of limbo dancers!

Illinois-Gregory Hall

(on condom dispenser) This gum tastes like rubber.

Illinois-Murphy's Bar

(arrow on window ledge pointing out window) Jump here!
Dead = A+; Critical = B; Broken leg = C; Broken nose = D; Little shook up = F.

Purdue-Main Library

(next to hole in the divider between study carrels)
List reasons for this hole:

       -practice plugging dikes
       -practice plugging dykes
       -honeymoon practice
       -one-fingered bowling ball
       -mold for donut hole
       -nose sizer
       -fresh air return
       -spy on couple next door
       -spittoon
       -see who rang door bell
       -ashtray
       -self-hypnotism
       -dildo steadier
       -to give disgusting minds something to turn
        on to
       -toe rest

Purdue-Main Library

Welcome to the throne-room of the porcelain god.

Wisconsin-Kollege Klub Bar

Ah yes, one of the greatest stimuli to the creativity of the Big Ten student is the toilet itself. Endless graffiti is written about this structure and the related bodily functions.

Some pieces are classics, found on each of the Big Ten campuses.

What are you looking up here for? You just pissed on your shoe.

Be like Dad, not like Sis,
lift the lid before you piss.

No matter how you stroke and dance,
the last few drops go down your pants.

One billion flies can't be wrong; eat shit!

Here I sit broken hearted,
tried to shit but only farted.
Yet better by far than risk the chance
to try to fart and crap my pants.

Flush twice; it's a long way to the cafeteria.

Please don't throw your cigarette butts in the stool; it
makes them soggy and most difficult to relight.

Here I sit in silent bliss,
listening to a telling piss.
Now and then a fart is heard,
followed by a dangling turd.

Here I sit in steamy vapor;
the ass before used all the paper.

Don't swim in our stools; we don't piss in your pools.

Don't put cigarette butts in the toilet; we don't shit in
your ashtrays.

Some come here to read and write.
Others come to wonder.
I come here to shit and piss,
and fart like fuckin' thunder.

(over urinal in men's restroom)
Be careful, the future of America is in your hands.

Some pieces of toilet graffiti are classics with a new twist.

What are you looking up here for? The joke's between your legs.

                -below-

It starts down there but it ends up here.

                                  Iowa-Phillips

Please remain seated through the entire performance.

                -below-

A word about the performance — it stunk!

                                  Iowa-Physics

Anyone can piss on the floor, but it takes a real man to shit on the ceiling.

                -below-

Not really . . . it's just a matter of sufficient pressure, correct viscosity, and a good ass-up aim.

                        Michigan-East Engineering

Still other pieces of graffiti have only their birthplace in common — the stalls and urinals of the Big Ten.

Welcome to Agronomy 673 - Manure Management.

                        Wisconsin-Agronomy

Ahhh . . . a contented flock of farts at play.

Northwestern-Technical Institute

(over urinal) Get a grip on yourself!

Iowa-Memorial Union

(on wall behind stool) If you're reading this, please go to the Student Health Services to have your head reversed.

Wisconsin-Memorial Library

No man is an island, but when you piss urination.

Michigan State-Erickson Hall

Save a tree; bring your own corncob.

Minnesota-Kolthoff Hall

Freedom's just another word for nothing left, too loose.

Wisconsin-Memorial Union

Ex-Lax makes me feel down and out.

Illinois-Lincoln Hall

Toulouse Lautrec is alive and well and living comfortably in this spacious compartment.

Indiana-Myers Hall

Here I sit on the pooper,
just gave birth to another State Trooper.

Wisconsin-White Library

Diarrhea is hereditary; it runs in your jeans.

Iowa-Memorial Union

It doesn't smell like tomato juice.

Wisconsin-Education

Please don't throw cigarette butts on the floor; the cockroaches are getting cancer.

Wisconsin-Law

(in toilet stall) This is an express line for people with seven items or less.

Michigan State-Library

Hi, Mom! Just in case I'm on camera.

Illinois-Library

All I really need is love, but a little toilet paper now and then would be nice.

Wisconsin-Zoology

Our aim is to keep this bathroom clean; your aim will help.

Indiana-Swain Hall

Here I sit infuriated,
strained to shit and nearly fainted.
Will have to leave contemplating
how to shit while regurgitating.
All because I'm constipated.

Michigan-Education

I'll bet I'm not the first man to shit in the ladies' restroom.

Ohio State-Union

(over urinals) Is this where all the pricks hang out?

Michigan State-Physics

That last plop was your wallet.
-below-
No, it was my pocket fisherman by Popeil.

Wisconsin-Botany

A full bladder gives you some time alone to realize how important your friends are.

Illinois-Murphy's Bar

Someone in here smells like a bus.

Indiana-Swain Hall

Do you ever wonder if there's a camera in the overhead light?

Wisconsin-Chemical Engineering

Is the past tense of 'shit', 'shat'?

Northwestern-Kresge Hall

I just fell in love with my hand.

Wisconsin-Chemical Engineering

1,000 turds = 1 kiloturd. Try dropping that on Hiroshima.

Ohio State-Smith Laboratory

Okay, who forgot to buy a newspaper for this stall?

Wisconsin-Chemical Engineering

Welcome to the Keebler cookie factory.

Indiana-Morrison Hall

Here I sit, buns a flexin'
giving birth to another Texan.

Illinois-Lincoln Hall

Drain your main vein and make your bladder gladder.

Wisconsin-Chemical Engineering

Constipation means never having to give a shit.

Michigan State-Physics

If you sprinkle when you tinkle, please be neat and wipe
the seat.

Northwestern-Lunt

Plop! Plop! Whiz! Whiz!
Oh, what a relief it is!

Wisconsin-Agriculture

Technique is everything.

Michigan-Library

*Several literary techniques used by the Big Ten graffitiist
are particularly suited to his art. These involve inspired re-
sponses to graffiti already written and may be retorts, postscripts,
supplements or addenda of assorted lengths.*

Why is there air?

        -below-

You ever tried breathing Cool Whip?

Ohio State-Thompson Library

Anyone know a good one-night stand?

-below-

What ya wanna stand for? Ya got a thing for phone booths?

Wisconsin-Social Science

For a good time call 665-1212

-below-

For a better time, masturbate.

Michigan-Hatcher Library

I gave it my all.

-below-

It sure didn't feel like it.

Ohio State-Thompson Library

Get out of Angola!

-below-

Who's she?

Minnesota-Aeronautic Engineering

Free Soviet Jews!

-below-

with each $25.00 purchase.

Northwestern-Technical Institute

The Clingons are coming!

-below-

If they're tall, dark and handsome they can cling on me.

Wisconsin-The Pub Bar

Anal sex is a pain in the ass.

-below-

But not as much as banal sex.

Indiana-Myers Hall

Butter is better!

-below-

than vaseline.

Minnesota-Zoology

Free Russian Jews!

-below-

Oh good! Can I get one?

Minnesota-Aeronautic Engineering

A misogynistic atheist; they're quite rare, you know.

-below-

Thank God!

Minnesota-Aeronautic Engineering

It's better to get pissed off than to get pissed on.

-below-

Have you ever been pissed on without being pissed off?

Illinois-Murphy's Bar

Save Soviet Jews!

-below-

Collect them or trade them with your friends.

Northwestern-Technical Institute

Fat people have more fun.

-below-

More fun than what, fat dogs?

Ohio State-Page Hall

Stop illegal aliens!

-below-

Mexicans or Martians?

Minnesota-Aeronautic Engineering

Adams was God's rough draft.

-below-

Leinenkugels is Wisconsin's smooth draft.

Wisconsin-White Library

Save Russian Jews!
> *-below-*

Win valuable prizes.

Wisconsin-History

I need a chick!
> *-below-*

Buy an egg!

Michigan-Little Science Lab

Jesus saves!
> *-below-*

But Esposito scores on rebounds!

Wisconsin-White Library

Ron is a cocksucking mother-fucking son-of-a-bitch!
> *-below-*

We must know the same Ron.
> *-below-*

It better not be the same Ron that I know. Ron's girl.
> *-below-*

It's the same Ron. Ron's mother.

Purdue-Library

Down with the Shah!
> *-below-*

I'd rather go down without him thanks.

Michigan-Hathcher Library

It's better to be rich and happy than to be poor and unhappy.

-below-

Are the poor so unhappy? Are the rich so happy?

-below-

I've been rich, and I've been poor. The rich are happier.

Michigan-Hatcher Library

I miss my Laura.

-below-

So do I.

-below-

So do all us L.A. Rams.

Iowa-Library

Everyone hates me because I'm paranoid.

-below-

Just because you're paranoid, don't think they don't hate you.

-below-

Everyone is paranoid because they all know I hate them.

Wisconsin-White Library

South Dakota: Where men are men and the sheep are nervous.

-below-

North Dakota: Where men are sheep and the women are nervous.

-below-

Washington D.C.: Where politicians are bought, the people
are nervous, and your secretaries tell.

Indiana-Swain Hall

Let's fuck, Honey!

    -below-

How does one fuck honey?

    -below-

A trifle messy, I'd wager.

                         Ohio State-Thompson Library

Ed loves Nancy.

    -below-

Nancy loves Ralph.

    -below-

I'm Ralph. Who is Nancy?

    -below-

I'm Ed, who is gonna punch Ralph for taking Nancy.

    -below-

I'm Tim, who is fucking Nancy while Ed punches Ralph.

    -below-

I'm Al, who is fucking Tim's girl while he's with Nancy.

    -below-

I'm Les, who loves Ralph but would like to meet Ed.

    -below-

Hi there! I'm Dave. I'm making a porno flick about this love triad and capitalizing on their wretched emotions.

                      Purdue-Library

$E = Mc^2$

    -below-

Good, Albert. Next time please submit your work papers.

    -below-

"Work papers": ~~$E=Mc^2$~~ ~~$E=Mc^2$~~ $E = Mc^2$

                      Wisconsin-Humanities

What is alert?

-below-

What? I wasn't paying attention.

-below-

A trumpet player.

-below-

It's a trela going backwards.

-below-

A person who lerts.

Michigan State-Engineering

Look at it this way — farts are shit without the mess.

-below-

They are easier to carry around and to get rid of.

-below-

They smell, so even the deaf can appreciate them.

-below-

They cut down on paperwork.

Minnesota-Zoology

Holly, come home. We miss you.

-below-

Ma

-below-

Pa

-below-

Gramps

-below-

Timmy

-below-

Lassie

Iowa-Engineering

Riddle me this, all you existential med students: How many amino acids can dance on the head of a pin?

     -below-

It depends on the music.

     -below-

How about "Pro-teen Angel?"

     -below-

Or, "It's Amino World?"

     -below-

Would you consider that acid rock?

          Indiana-Myers Hall

Why must one go to a university for four years to become unemployed?

     -below-

To enhance the status of unemployment.

     -below-

To learn to accept rejection.

     -below-

For alumni events.

     -below-

To meet preppy bitches.

     -below-

To abuse drugs.

     -below-

To learn the true merits of vocational training.

        Wisconsin-Social Science

Please remember today's lesson. "Bullwinkle is . . ."

     -below-

How a cow knows for sure.

       Indiana-T.V. and Broadcasting

World's shortest list:
>   *-below-*
creative accountants
>   *-below-*
good American cars
>   *-below-*
qualified campus security officers
>   *-below-*
chicanos I have met while yachting
>   *-below-*
Italian war heroes
>   *-below-*
graffitiists who can spell rite
>   *-below-*
this list two months ago
>   *-below-*
consecutive winning seasons at Iowa

>   *Iowa-Phillips Hall*

I wanted to be a pathologist, but it was a deadend job.
>   *-below-*
I wanted to be a surgeon, but I wasn't cut out for it.
>   *-below-*
I wanted to be a plumber, but it wasn't fitting.
>   *-below-*
I wanted to be an electrician, but the idea shocked me.
>   *-below-*
I wanted to be in the Air Force, but the idea bombed.
>   *-below-*
I wanted to be a cook, but I got burned.
>   *-below-*
I wanted to be a photographer, but nothing developed.
>   *-below-*

I wanted to be a gambler, but the odds were against me.

        -below-

I wanted to be a dairy farmer, but I was an udder failure.

        -below-

I wanted to be a drug runner, but it was a dopey idea.

        -below-

I wanted to be a male prostitute, but I couldn't get up for it.

        -below-

I wanted to be a comedian, but I couldn't Hackett.

        -below-

I wanted to be a fisherman, but I got hooked on something else.

        -below-

I wanted to be an arsonist, but couldn't get fired up for it.

        -below-

I wanted to be a doctor, but didn't have any patience.

        -below-

I wanted to be an asshole, butt. . .

        -below-

My friend wanted to be an asshole, but the prospects rectum.

        Minnesota-Zoology

Emb, Ariz.	Frito, La.
Idunno, Alaska	Good, La.
Fount, Tenn.	Trala, La.
Marcuswelby, Md.	Praise, Ala.
Ball Point, Penn.	Iam, Ill.
Ell, S.D.	Koh, Tex.
Amosen, N.D.	Singalongwith, Mich.
Wonder, N.Y.	Critical, Mass.
Sprayin, Wash.	
Vita, Minn.	
Noaz, Ark.	
Eim, Ok.	
Eenymeenymynny, Mo.	*Wisconsin-English*

The limerick form is complex...

No collection of graffiti could be complete without the limerick form.

The limerick form is complex.
Its contents run chiefly to sex.
It burgeons with virgins
and masculine urgin's
and swarms with erotic effects.

Wisconsin-South Hall

A craftsman who weaves in Khartuom
lures very young boys to his room.
Consumed by a beaver,
this Sudanese weaver
was nicknamed "the fruit of the loom."

Minnesota-Zoology

There once was a gaucho named Bruno
who said, "Fucking is one thing I do know.
Sheep are just fine.
Women devine.
But llama are numero uno."

Wisconsin-Social Science

A bisexual caveman named Roy
befriended a longhaired young boy.
The boy thought it fair
to be dragged by his hair,
but the club up his ass was no joy.

Minnesota-Smith Hall

In the Garden of Eden lay Adam
complacently stroking his madam.
And great was his mirth
for he knew that on Earth
there were only two balls, and he had 'em.

Wisconsin-Chemical Engineering

There once was fellow named Dick
who perfected a wonderful trick.
He'd get an erection
and scorn all protection
and balance himself on his prick.

Minnesota-Murphy Hall

There once was a fellow from Kent
whose dick was so long it was bent.
He got into trouble
when he put it in double;
instead of coming it went.

Indiana-Memorial Hall

There once was a hooker named Sue
who filled her vagina with glue.
When they paid to get in
she said with a grin,
"You must pay to get out of it too."

Minnesota-Murphy Hall

There once was a harlot from Yale
who had prices engraved on her tail,
and on her behind
for the use of the blind
each was repeated in braille.

Purdue-Library

There once was a girl from Detroit
who at fucking herself was adroit.
She said with a grin
as the dildo went in,
"You had better believe I enjoy it."

Minnesota-Murphy Hall

A timorous Viking name Kord
got seasick whenever aboard,
until Princess Vale
enticed him to sail
his longboat the length of her fjord.

Northwestern-Technical Institute

There was young lady from Wheeling
who said she had no sexual feeling,
but a fellow named Boris
did lick her clitoris,
and she had to be scraped off the ceiling.

Minnesota-Zoology

The baker's apprentice named Ned
could coax not a maiden to bed
until they discerned
the tricks he had learned
while kneading the dough for the bread.

Ohio State-Thompson Library

There once was a lady named Gail
who loved to sit down on a nail.
Her friends often wondered
if she ever blundered
and ever quite failed to impale.

Minnesota-Murphy Hall

There once was a man named Sinclair
who was fucking his girl on the stair.
The bannister broke
and he quickened his stroke
and finished her off in mid air.

Purdue-Library

A young trapeze artist named Bract
is faced with a very sad fact —
imagine his pain
when, again and again,
he catches his wife in the act.

Minnesota-Zoology

There once was monk from Algeria
whose knowledge was somewhat inferior.
One night of fun
with a comely young nun,
and now she's a Mother Superior.

Wisconsin-Law

A newlywed couple named Kelly
spent their honeymoon belly to belly,
because in their haste
they used library paste
instead of petroleum jelly.

Minnesota-Vincent Hall

There was a young man named Hope
who often fucked an oscilloscope.
The cyclical trace
of their carnal embrace
had damn near infinite slope.

Michigan State-Giltner Hall

There once was fellow named Frisk
whose stroke was exceedingly brisk.
So fast was his action
that the Lorenz contraction
reduced his tool to a disk.

Michigan-East Engineering

According to experts, the oyster
in its shell (a crustacean cloister)
may frequently be
either he or a she
or both, if it should be its choice ter.

Minnesota-Zoology

Reality is far better when it is shared.

Wisconsin-Chemical Engineering

Big Ten graffiti is not without its poignancy.

I wish someone loved me; no one does.

        -below-

Someone will soon.

        Ohio State-Union

Could I be more like you?

        Iowa-Physics

I wish I had a moment, a day, a year or even a life time. . .
to think not of who I am or what I'll do, but why I am here.

Purdue-Library

Why is it that education causes stress? Why must school be
so presumed? Competition so intense?

-below-

Because you let it worry you. Lighten up.

Michigan-Hatcher Library

But I never lost my pride.

-below-

In doing that, did you damage anyone else's?

Michigan-Hatcher Library

Can't we still be friends?

Iowa-Gilmore Hall

Some peope's lives are lives of quiet desperation. Take
mine for instance . . . please.

-below-

How about if I just shove a grenade up your ass.

Indiana-Ballantine Hall

Some days you just can't win.

Michigan-Hatcher Library

Ever have one of those days when even your nose hairs
stab you?

Minnesota-Engineering

I've got a test, and I'm scared shitless.

Indiana-Swain Hall

Weekend, where are you?

Purdue-Library

I've got the L.A. blues again.

Wisconsin-Agriculture

I need a friend — someone who understands me and has time
to be there and time to listen when I need someone; one who is
willing to share the good times and bad times with me; someone
to just love me and be my friend.

Ohio State-Thompson Library

Christ! I'm so mixed up and lonely I can't even make friends
with my mind. I'm too young to be where I'm going, and too old
to go back again.

Wisconsin-Social Science

Everyone I know is anonymous.

Northwestern-Harris Hall

Nobody loves me; everybody hates me. I think I'll go and
eat a can of worms.

Purdue-Library

I need someone to love me and help me to become what I want
to be and help me do what I want in life.

Ohio State-Thompson Library

I'm afraid to live.
I'm afraid to die.
I'm afraid.
I'm sorry for the bad things I've done in my life.
I wish I could win,
but I always seem to be a loser.
I'm afraid.

Purdue-Library

What concerns me is that nothing concerns me.

Wisconsin-Social Science

I'd rather madness to this sadness in my brain.

Northwestern-Swift Hall

If all my thoughts are me, my mind's going off its hinges.

Michigan-Hatcher Library

I should be spontaneously abolished.

Ohio State-Thompson Library

I was aborted.

Ohio State-Thompson Library

Too many martyrs, too many dead

Illinois-Fine Arts

Things are looking brighter.

Michigan-Hatcher Library

Sitting quietly doing nothing.   Spring comes and the grass
grows by itself.

Illinois-Lincoln Hall

I'm getting married!   Wow!   I can't believe it!

Ohio State-Union

I just got accepted to dental school!

-below-

Good for you!

Purdue-Library

Don't tell me this world has no heart.

Indiana-Memorial Union

A little coitus never hoitus!

Indiana-Memorial Union

It will probably come as a surprise to few that a considerable portion of the graffiti of Big Ten students had to do with sex. The following chapters devote themselves to the various aspects of that topic.

Sex is like a snowstorm — you never know how many inches you'll get or how long it will last.

Indiana-Mason Hall

Sex is like the game of euchre — if you've got a good hand you might as well go it alone.

Michigan-East Engineering

At least masturbation is sex with someone you love.

Wisconsin-Social Science

Contraceptives should be used at every conceivable occasion.

Michigan-East Engineering

Saran Wrap — #1 at Michigan!
        Tear if off!
        Wrap it up!
        Stick it in!

Michigan-West Engineering

In days of old when knights were bold
and rubbers weren't invented,
they laid a sock
across their cock,
and babies were prevented.

Indiana-Myers Hall

Virginity is not something to be ashamed of, just cured.

Minnesota-Zoology

Virginity is a birth defect. Give generously to wipe it out.

Michigan State-Giltner Hall

Virginity is like a bubble — one prick and it's gone.

Michigan State-Giltner Hall

If it hurts you're probably doing it the wrong way.

Iowa-Phillips Hall

People who think sex is a pain in the ass should turn over.

Purdue-Library

There is nothing as over-rated as a good fuck and nothing so under-rated as a good shit.

Indiana-Myers Hall

The sexual life cycle of a male: tri-weekly, try weekly, try weakly.

Illinois-Lincoln Hall

I gave up bowling for sex — the balls are lighter and I don't have to wear shoes.

Northwestern-University Hall

If you think any sex is free you haven't had any.

Minnesota-Vincent Hall

Remember: Sex can lead to marriage, and in serious cases there have been reports of babies.

Purdue-Library

Attention!!! You may be having sex and not even know it! Here are three early warning signs:
1. sudden peeling of the clothes
2. sweaty palms
3. a guilty feeling when you wake up in the morning

Purdue-Library

If you eat corn chips while fucking, does that mean you have Frito lays?

Minnesota-Tate Laboratories

Necrophilia is a dead act.

Indiana-Myers Hall

Incest is relative.

Michigan State-Natural Sciences

If a ram is a sheep and as ass is a donkey, how come a ram in the ass is a goose?

Michigan State-Giltner Hall

It's better to wear out than rust out.

Michigan State-Library

If Hite is right, thrusting is sheer phallacy.

Minnesota-Zoology

Oh, George, let's not park here.
"   "   "   "   "
"   "   "   "
"   "   "
"   "
"

Minnesota-Murphy Hall

She offered her honor.
I honored her offer.
So all night long
it was on her and off her.

Classic on all campuses

Jack and Jill worked at the mill
until the work did slack.
The miller cried,
"I can't decide
whether to lay Jill or Jack off."

Iowa-Basic Sciences

It is better to have loved and lost, than to have paid
for it and not liked it.

Minnesota-Walter Library

Crunch taco balls.   Eat a macho man.

Illinois-Murphy's Bar

It's good to find a hard man.

Michigan-Hatcher Library

Roses are red.   Violets are blue.
You don't know beauty 'til there's 10" in you.

Wisconsin-Porta Bella Restaurant

Do something big; fuck a giant.

Wisconsin-White Library

For a good time, call . . .

Classic on all campuses.

For an adequate time call 277-3321.

Wisconsin-The Pub Bar

269-7221 — You can call, but no promises.

Michigan State-Library

For a good suck, buy a Kirby.

Michigan State-Engineering

For a close encounter of the fourth kind, call . . .

Ohio State-Thompson Library

If a physically impressive young man would like a non-stop,
no-holds-barred physically refreshing sexual relationship with a

junior Purdue female, address a personals in the Exponent to Alice.
Satisfaction guaranteed!

Purdue-Library

Girls! Jump into Spring with a bang! Let Stanley's Stud
Services do it for you! Our staff of well-trained studs consists
of: 13 basketball players
         5 swim team members
         3 bodybuilders
         2 burnouts
         1 fag

Ohio State-Hatcher Library

Women of Purdue! If you have trouble achieving a satis-
fying orgasm, I have the answer. If you would like a back-to-
back double shattering orgasm, call the oral sex king.
"Butterfly Flick" Rick at 742-6013.
Also game for anal intercourse, group sex and S&M (mild).

Purdue-Library

Pardon my hard-on.

Iowa-Library

Weenies make better lovers!

Northwestern-Technical Institute

A cock is like a sock — if it's too small it's of no use, it it's too big it sags down your leg.

Wisconsin-425 Henry Mall

Why do women have trouble telling distances? Because they are constantly told that a six inch penis is really a foot.

Michigan-Little Science Building

Nothing is more difficult than trying to explain to your wife how you got teeth marks on your cock.

Minnesota-Zoology

I have finally devised a way to make my penis two feet long — fold it in half.

Minnesota-Zoology

My cock is eight inches long. Let's see you beat that!
            -below-
No thanks. I'm sure you can beat it yourself.

Minnesota-Zoology

I may be slow, but the ladies like it.

Minnesota-Engineering

I get more ass than this toilet seat.

Iowa-Physics

It's not how long you make it, but how you make it long.

Minnesota-Zoology

Archivists make it last longer.

Wisconsin-Education

Iowa–Library

All I need is a good fuck to set my head straight.

Michigan–Hatcher Library

I need a cranium job!

Iowa–Airliner Bar

I need a woman 'bout twice my age.

Illinois–Lincoln Hall

I'm so horny the crack of dawn had better watch out.

Iowa–Engineering

Sex is a misdemeanor;   the more I miss, the meaner I get.

Ohio State-Thompson Library

Horny?   Take matters into your own hands.

Indiana-Swain Hall

Women are like stamps -
you lick 'em, stick 'em
and send 'em away.

Iowa-Engineering

All of us are on the hunt,
looking for some juicy cunt.

Michigan State-Giltner Hall

Round like an apple,
plump as a pear,
with a slit in the middle,
all covered with hair — a peach.

Ohio State-Hopkins Hall

Panties may not be the best thing in the world, but they're
the next thing to it.

Michigan-Business Administration

I'd walk a mile
for a vertical smile.

Ohio State-Thompson Library

The bearded clam is the natural prey of the one-eyed
trouser snake.

Michigan-Union

Be kind to a beaver — plant a post it its habitat.

Minnesota-Zoology

Hello, girl! Your supper's waiting for you.

Michigan-Hatcher Library

If she swallows it, she loves you.

Michigan State-Horticulture Eng.

If God hadn't meant for us to suck cock, why'd he make it
look like a popcicle?

Wisconsin-Social Science

Eat pussy, not grapes!

Michigan State-Library

If God hadn't meant Man to eat pussy he wouldn't have made it look like a taco.

Wisconsin-Van Hise Hall

Take a taco to lunch.

Michigan State-Giltner Hall

Follicle pie is the way to fly.
The joys of the tongue are too unsung.

Michigan State-Engineering

Let's play carnival — you sit on my face and I'll guess your weight.

Ohio State-Page Hall

The problem is the clitoris; together we can lick it.

Michigan-East Engineering

Stimulate a clitoris today!

Minnesota-Vincent Hall

Only two things smell like fish — one is fish.

Wisconsin-White Library

If girls are made of sugar and spice, how come they taste
like tuna fish?

Michigan State-Engineering

Ohio State's #1 Sport: muff diving

Ohio State-Thompson Library

It's Spring! I love the flowers and the birds and the
bare tits.

Iowa-Chemistry & Botany

Guys don't make passes
at girls with fat asses.

Northwestern-University Hall

Fat-bottomed girls, they make this rockin' world go 'round.

Indiana-Myers Hall

I need a respectable girl.
    -below-
I respect a needed girl.

Purdue-Library

Puberty is when a girl's voice changes from "No" to "Yes".

Michigan-East Engineering

Okay, men, get 'em while they're hot!

Northwestern-Technical Institute

Stoke 'er 'fore she gets cold!

Iowa-Gilmore Hall

It is more pleasurable to kiss a virgin than to fuck a slut.

Wisconsin-Music

Women are like screen doors — the more you bang 'em, the looser they get.

Michigan State-Physics

Bang one girl, you've banged 'em all.

Purdue-Library

Venus never farted!

Wisconsin-Humanities

Negative temperatures exist and are alive and well in spin systems and preppy bitches.

Michigan-Little Science Building

Why Northwestern coeds are not like toilet seats:
-toilet seats warm up when you touch them
-holes in toilet seats don't get stretched out
-toilet seats take a lot of shit without complaining
-toilet seats are easier to pick up, and won't let you
   down or stand you up.

Northwestern-Education

Differences between U of Michigan girls and toilet seats:
-toilet seats don't have droopy boobs
-you can get used to the looks of a toilet seat
-toilet seats warm up when you touch them
-toilet seats are always there when you need them
-you can talk to toilet seats
-toilet seats don't bitch
-toilet seats always go down for you
-toilet seats don't get headaches
-toilet seats never say, "It's my time of the month."
-you don't have to kiss a toilet seat to use it
-toilet seats like it when you talk dirty to them

Michigan-West Engineering

She said, "Give me sex and make it hurt."
So I licked her tit and punched her in the mouth.

Illinois-Gregory Hall

This filth on bathroom walls is the direct cause of female subjugation.

Indiana-Rawles Hall

Sex is the husband's pleasure and the wife's duty.

Wisconsin-Social Science

Go sexual revolution! Cast away those Judeo-Christian morals!

Illinois-Undergraduate Library

Behind every successful man is a fish with a bicycle.

Wisconsin-White Library

What's with all these penises on the wall?
-below-
They're easier to draw than a pair of lips and a vagina,
I guess.

Wisconsin-Social Science

This bathroom is womanspace. It is where we come together
and communicate with each other without the ever-present men.

Wisconsin-YMCA

If you're so liberated, why doesn't he sleep on the wet spot?
-below-
Disgusting!
-below-
What wet spot?

Wisconsin-Spudnuts Restaurant

Make her sleep on the wet spot!

Ohio State-Denny Hall

In all reality, she should sleep on the wet spot.
-below-
But there's no dry spot for me.
-below-
Sleep with it between your legs.

Iowa-AV Pizza Villa

Love is all you need.
                    -below-
Sex is all you get.

                              Wisconsin-Commerce

When will I be loved?
                    -below-
When the price is right.

                              Wisconsin-White Library

Love and sex aren't mutually exclusive, are they?

Wisconsin-Humanities

Love will get you through times of no sex better than sex will get you through times of no love.

Illinois-Murphy's Bar

To be loved is all I need, and whom I love, I love indeed.

Wisconsin-425 Henry Mall

I think I'm in love.

-below-

If you have to think, you're not.

Illinois-Undergraduate Library

I'm madly in liking with Jeff!

Illinois-Undergraduate Library

I need to know how to French kiss by Friday night, any hints?

Wisconsin-Commerce

Just give me a man with a million or two,
or one that is cute would happily do.
But if the man shortage should get any worse,
go back to the first line of my little verse —
Just give me a man . . .

Purdue-Library

It must have been the roses, the roses or the ribbons in
her long brown hair.

Michigan-Hatcher Library

V.D. is nothing to clap about.

Purdue-Library

No need to stand on the seat — I.U. crabs can jump three feet.

Indiana-Morrison Hall

Please don't flush toothpicks, the crabs can pole vault.

Iowa-Engineering

Get rid of crabs! Find someone who loves seafood.

Wisconsin-Memorial Union

V.D. can be licked!

Minnesota-Zoology

95

Heterosexuals are people too!

Wisconsin-White Library

Homosexuality is a rumor perpetrated by Masters and Johnson.

Michigan-Little Science Building

Gay is the way!
                -below-
Hetero is better though.

Michigan-Mason Hall

God made rivers.
God made snakes.
When God made gays
He made mistakes.

Michigan-Union

Fags begone!

-below-

With diamond earrings and white leather shoulder bag.

Michigan-Hatcher Library

Don't hunt harp seals; beat faggots!

-below-

Or at least paint them in wild colors so they know each
other's faggot asses and don't fag with normal folks.

Michigan State-Giltner Hall

A fuck a day and you'll never be gay.

Michigan State-Chemistry

Greek is gay!

Northwestern-Technical Institute

Frat boys get it in the end.

Northwestern-Technical Institute

Since homosexuals can't produce viable offspring, why worry?

Indiana-Fine Arts

Oh Mary, conceived without sin,
help us sin without conceiving.

-below-

Making love with another woman would be a good answer to
this problem, but it isn't an answer because it is not a sin.

Wisconsin-Social Science

Gay sex is better
than bi-sex or hetter.

Wisconsin-Porta Bella Restaurant

We are all basically bisexual.

Wisconsin-Commerce

By and by we are all bi.

Wisconsin-White Library

Beastiality is never having to say you're sorry.

Wisconsin-Music

Roses are red. Violets are blue.
The dog is pregnant, thanks to you.

Michigan-Union

The problem with fucking a cow is that you have to get on
your back to suck her tits and run around front to kiss her.

Michigan State-Agriculture

Mary had a little sheep.
But when dear Mary went to sleep
the sheep turned out to be a ram,
so Mary had a little lamb.

Minnesota-Zoology

I like sheep!

Michigan-Undergraduate Library

It's me and ewe, baby!

Northwestern-Technical Institute

REALITY is for those who can't handle DRUGS.

Classic on all campuses.

Sex and drugs and rock-n-roll are all I need.

Ohio State-Thompson Library

If you loved something you wouldn't need drugs and alcohol.
-below-
I do love something — I love drugs and alcohol!

Michigan State-Engineering

God made pot, and God made beer.
In God we trust.

Michigan State-North Kedzie

Open your eyes,
you'll get a surprise.
Evil is sweeping the nation.
It's killing your sons,
and not only your sons,
your daughters are out for sensation.
When they turn on
their mothers are gone,
they don't even know what they're doing.
It's a dangerous craze,
a teenage malaise,
leaving them hearts of ruin.
Reefer Madness has stolen our children.

Northwestern-Swift Hall

If dope is a crutch, the world has a broken leg.

Illinois-Gregory Hall

Drugs are a reality for those who can't handle crutches.

Iowa-Art

Reality — love it or leave it!

Iowa-Airliner Bar

Drugs are the essence of things hoped for, and the evidence
of things unseen.

Michigan-Hatcher Library

Take a peek at your mind.

Michigan-Hatcher Library

Grass is Nature's way of saying, "High."

Wisconsin-Chemical Engineering

Breed pot, not plutonium!

Wisconsin-Memorial Union

Good ol' Iowa ditch!

Iowa-Physics

Not much pot is grown by Swiss, but every little bit Alps.

Indiana-Rawles Hall

Paraquat! Breakfast of champions!

Michigan-Undergraduate Library

Roll, roll, roll a joint.
Pass it down the line.
Toke, toke, hold the smoke.
Blow your fucking mind.

Wisconsin-Geology

A joint a day keeps reality away.

Wisconsin-YMCA

Hither come to suck a pipe
and turn my brain to cheese and tripe.
Celebrate while sucking bong,
commence to coughing all night long.

Minnesota-Smith Hall

If you want to get high on pot, stand on the toilet seat.

Michigan State-Engineering

Prometheus got stoned — but why not, he gave everyone else
a light first.

Wisconsin-White Hall

Smoke Yumbo!

Minnesota-Walter Library

LSD is the playground of your mind.

Michigan-Business Administration

Acid consumes 47 times its weight in excess reality.

Indiana-Morrison Hall

LSD melts your mind, not your hand.

Wisconsin-YMCA

Long Slow Death!

Michigan-Undergraduate Library

Don't drop acid — take it pass/fail.

Iowa-Physics

Cocaine — the thinking man's Dristan.

Michigan-Mason Hall

Cocaine is for horses and not for men.
They say it will kill you, but they don't say when.

Iowa-Chemistry & Botany

Give me librium, or give me death!

Wisconsin-Parthenon Restaurant

A bottle of white. a bottle of red.
Maybe a bottle of rose' instead.

Ohio State-Thompson Library

I think that I shall never hear
a poem as lovely as a beer.
That good ol' brew tastes best on tap
with its golden base and snowy cap.
That lovely stuff I drink all day
until my memory melts away.
Poems are made by fools I fear,
but only Schlitz can make a beer.

Ohio State-Thompson

Not drunk is he who from the floor
can rise alone and drink some more.
But drunk is he who prostrate lies
without the strength to drink or rise.

Michigan-Hatcher Library

I used to be a smoker.
Man, it was lots of fun.
And then something happened,
I almost lost a lung.

Now I'm not a smoker,
but I really like to chew.
So don't blow your smoke at me
and I won't spit at you.

Iowa-Gilmore Hall

Smokers! Tell us when you're in intensive care with emphysema,
draining shit from your lungs. We'll come over and have a barbeque
in your room.

Minnesota-Vincent Hall

Politics is like a steer.

Indiana-Balantine Hall

The trouble with America is that so many political jokes get elected.

Wisconsin-Humanities

If 'pro' is the opposite of 'con', what is the opposite of progress?

Wisconsin-Memorial Union

The difference between Republicans and Democrats is the difference between syphilis and gonorrhea.

Michigan State-Erickson Hall

You can't shit here, your asshole is in Washington D.C.

Iowa-Phillips

Re-elect Jimmy Carter, the best president Panama ever had.

Illinois-Lincoln Hall

Carter is living proof that mountain men screwed buffaloes.

Wisconsin-Memorial Union

Jimmy Carter - one in a million.
Billy Carter - one in four.

Minnesota-Zoology

Jimmy Carter — public enema #1.

Wisconsin-Parthenon Restaurant

Who has the biggest boobs in Washington D.C.?
Miss Lillian — Jimmy and Billy.

Wisconsin-Law

Nixon is an honest man. No one believes me; I'm pissed!

Ohio State-Thompson Library

Dick Nixon before he dicks you.

Indiana-Myers Hall

Teddy can help us "bridge" our differences.

Iowa-Phillips Hall

Nixon saw Deep Throat ten times and still couldn't get it down Pat.

Wisconsin-White Hall

Nixon did for America what panty hose did for finger fucking.

Wisconsin-Chemical Engineering

Woody and Nixon in 1980. Help bring us together again.

Ohio State-Thompson Library

I like Ike!

Minnesota-Zoology

Bring back the spirit of the Sixties. Bring back the way we stood up for our rights and got involved in what was going on.

Indiana-Memorial Union

If you didn't vote, don't complain.

-below-

If you didn't complain, don't vote.

Wisconsin-Union South

Fighting for peace is like fucking for virginity.

Classic on all campuses

If the draft comes back, I'm taking names for a bus to Canada.

Michigan State-Chemistry

One solution to the class struggle — eat and shit the rich.

Wisconsin-Memorial Library

Join the I.W.W. and get back at your boss.

-below-

Form a collective and get rid of your boss.

Wisconsin-YMCA

Workers of the world rise up!

-below-

So that we can more easily gun you down.

Wisconsin-Social Science

The difference between Communism and Capitalism is that under Capitalism man exploits man, and under Communism it's the other way around.

Wisconsin-Economics

Don't be a dummy, be a smartie.
Come and join the Nazi Party.

Michigan State-Engineering

If you think Hitler is dead, two weeks in Buenos Aires should change your mind.

Ohio State-Dulles Hall

More power to the right wing! (a patriot)
-below-
Which will result in a left turn! (a pilot)

Wisconsin-Social Science

Give America back to the Indians!
-below-
Give India back to the Americans!

Wisconsin-Memorial Union

Send the Nationalists back to China!

Wisconsin-Social Science

Taiwan for the Taiwanese!

Wisconsin-Social Science

U.S. out of North America!

Wisconsin-Social Science

Down with shades! Down with shelves!
Down with Snow White and her elves!

Indiana-Memorial Union

Free Puerto Rico!
> *-below-*

No way! Where would we get our baseball players from?

Wisconsin-Social Science

Down with Babylon!
> *-below-*

No more hanging gardens!
> *-below-*

Hang the King, not the gardens! (the people)
> *-below-*

The King is already quite well hung. (the Queen)
> *-below-*

Babylon is reality! Bethlehem is the dream!

Wisconsin-Memorial Library

Before the Jews, Israel was a bunch of desert-roaming nomads. Now that it's developed you want it back to let your camels shit.

Indiana-Memorial Union

Why are there so many Iranian students here fighting their revolution? Why aren't they home if they're so brave and tough?

Indiana-Ballantine Hall

Iranian students give Communism a bad name.

Michigan-Mason Hall

Let's not lose Iran to the Commies!

Ohio State-Thompson Library

Long live Iran!
        -below-
Go bugger a bedouin!

Illinois-Library

Long live the Shah!
        -below-
Somewhere other than Iran or the United States.

Michigan State-Chemistry

Return the Shah!

-below-

Along with 50,000 Marines!

Northwestern-Technical Institute

Thanks to the environmentalists we can all sniff clean air while we starve to death.

Michigan-East Engineering

Can nuclear power give you whiter teeth?
You bet your life!

Wisconsin-YMCA

Recall Simonsen!

-below-

Yeah, I recall him. Horrible fellow, wasn't he.

Wisconsin-Memorial Library

If this is a free country, why are we paying so much for it?

Wisconsin-Humanities

Bigotry is hard to remove
from a man. It wasn't
reasoned in, and it can't
be reasoned out.

Michigan State-Engineering

*Unfortunately, bigotry too is a part of the graffiti of the
Big Ten student.*

Midwesterners are merely an advanced species of apes.
    -below-
Whereas, Easterners are a primitive species.

Wisconsin-Botany

American security is racial purity.

Michigan State-Engineering

WASP's are living proof of what Pilgrims did with turkeys.

Ohio State-Thompson Library

Affirmative action is for inferiors.

Ohio State-Thompson Library

Institute white quotas for basketball teams.

Michigan-East Engineering

Iranians are living proof of Attila the Hun's affection for water buffalo.

Ohio State-Undergraduate Library

The remainder of this page and the two following pages were expurgated to remove bigoted graffiti of no redeeming value.

*We had planned to include the appropriate proportion
of representative graffiti of this ilk to show that the
Big Ten was not exempt from such outpourings of nastiness.
However, we decided that that point could be made by
simply stating it.*

It is as stated in the chapter title — "Bigotry is
hard to remove from a man. It wasn't reasoned in, and it
can't be reasoned out."

```
*   *   *   *   *   *   *   *   *   *   *   *

*                                           *
        Additional copies of "Graffiti
*    In The Big Ten" may be acquired at     *
     your local bookstore or by sending
*    $4.50 per copy to:                      *

*                                           *
     Brown House Galleries
*    Dept. 1                                 *

*    P.O. Box 4243                           *
     Madison, WI 53711
*                                           *

*   *   *   *   *   *   *   *   *   *   *   *
```

Why hasn't GOD returned my calls?

Sometimes the thoughts of the Big Ten graffitiists went to a higher level.

I need a shot of salvation!

Sinners, resoul thyself!

The day of judgement is upon us. Repent!

-below-

No, repeat!

Iowa-Gilmore Hall

Smile, Jesus loves you.

-below-

Smile, you're being fooled again.

Ohio State-Thompson Library

Jesus smoked pot when she walked across the water.

Wisconsin-YMCA

Jesus is coming, and is he pissed.

-below-

If he is, then he's a slow learner.

Ohio State-Hopkins Hall

If Jesus was a Jew, why'd he have a Puerto Rican name?

Northwestern-Fisk Hall

Why wasn't Jesus born in Ohio? Because when God went there
he couldn't find three wise men or a virgin.

Michigan State-Agriculture

God didn't create the world in seven days. He partied for six days and pulled an all-nighter.

Classic on all campuses

A woman without God is like a frog without a bicycle.

Wisconsin-Social Science

God has a bicycle.

Wisconsin-White Library

God may be dead, but the Virgin Mary is pregnant again.

Classic on all campuses

God may be dead, but 50,000 social workers have risen to take his place.

Wisconsin-425 Henry Mall

God helps those who got the price of a ticket.

Wisconsin-Social Science

Don't go mistaking paradise with that house across the road.

Indiana-Political Science

Pope John Paul I — The patron saint of the "limited-term employees."

Wisconsin-Club de Wash

Jesus saves!
-below-
Moses invests!
-below-
Mohammed owns the bank!
-below-
No, Rockefeller owns the bank and he has frozen Mohammed's assets.

Wisconsin-Social Science

Are you ready
to become
a planetary
citizen?

Wisconsin-White Library

And sometimes Big Ten graffiti is out of this world.

It is my distinct impression that most people could benefit by reading a Rand McNally Intergalactic Map.

Minnesota-Tate Laboratories

Scottie! Beam me up!

Wisconsin-White Library

Let's not lose Mars to the Commies.

Illinois-Undergraduate Library

Bomb Mars now!

Iowa-Phillips Hall

Beam us up, Scottie!   No sign of intelligent life down here.

Minnesota-Vincent Hall

I've been all over this universe, and take my word for it, Earth makes the best popcorn.

Minnesota-Walter Library

Earth's under the weather.

Wisconsin-Humanities

Beam me up, Scottie!

-below-

Ya canna deny the laws of physics, Cap'n.   I got to have thirty minutes.

-below-

He's dead, Jim!

Minnesota-Agriculture

We're all partners in the cosmic dance.

Ohio State-Lord Hall

What is a cosmic giggle?

Ohio State-Hopkins Hall

More power, Scottie!
-below-
I'm sorry, Cap'n, but she's at warp nine already and canna take no more.

Illinois-Lincoln Hall

We have just discovered an important message from space — the Martians plan to throw a dance for the Human Race.

Minnesota-Smith Hall

Beam me up, Scottie!
-below-
I canna do it, Cap'n. The beam is broken and the negative warp drive is increasing.

Minnesota-Engineering

I'd like to see Uranus.

Iowa-Phillips

The world is looking back at you.

Illinois-Lincoln Hall

Beam me up, Scottie!
-below-
I canna do it, Cap'n. You're surrounded by steamy vapors
that are causin' a disengagement of the transmitter ray.
-below-
Any ideas, Spock?
-below-
Try another stall, and this time don't fart.

Michigan-Pharmacy Building

Believe in the invisible ray!
-below-
That's true; I haven't seen Ray in weeks.

Wisconsin-YMCA

The Moon may be smaller than Earth, but it's further away.

Michigan-Hatcher Library

Nano! Nano!

Purdue-Library

May the bird of paradise nose up your fly!

Minnesota-Zoology

Big Ten students often leave affectionate messages for their friends.

May a buffalo in heat find you in his time of need!
Indiana-Myers Hall

May poisonous snakes dwell in the corners of your cupboards!
Michigan-Business Administration

May your pen drop from your syphilitic fingers!

Purdue-Library

May you be run over by a wheelchair basketball team!

Michigan-Little Science Building

Up your nose with a rubber hose!

-below-

Up your ass with a piece of glass!

Michigan-Business Adminstration

Eat a flaming frisbee!

Iowa-Library

Did you hear the one about...

There were jokes — some good, some . . .

Did you hear about the Acapulco hooker who gave such good head that she was called the Gulp of Mexico.

Minnesota-Zoology

Why do they boil water when delivering a baby?
So that if it is born dead they can make soup.

Wisconsin-Chemical Engineering

What's the difference between a girl's track team and some smart pygmies? One is a bunch of cunning runts.

Indiana-Myers Hall

How is the military like a rubber?
They both give you the feeling of protection while you're getting fucked.

Ohio State-Cockins Hall

Why did the Polish woman stop breast feeding her baby?
It hurt too much when she boiled her nipples.
>   *-below-*
After two feedings she ran out of breasts.

Michigan State-Horticulture Eng.

How many Californians does it take to replace a light bulb?
Eight, one to turn the bulb and seven to share the experience.

Michigan-Business Administration

What is Arthur Fiedler doing now?
Decomposing.

Harvard-Physics
(visiting scholar contribution)

Why did Helen Keller masturbate with one hand?
So she could groan with the other.

Michigan-Business Adminstration

What do you serve a thirsty ghost?
Ghoul-ade.

Wisconsin-Education

What is red and green and goes 500 miles per hour?
A frog in a blender.

Wisconsin-Education

How do you separate the men from the boys in the Greek Army?
With a crowbar.

Wisconsin-Parthenon Restaurant

What do a Polish girl and a hockey player have in common?
They both wear their pads for three periods.

Illinois-Gregory Hall

How did Hitler tie his shoes?
In little knotsies.

Wisconsin-Union South

What's red, white and blue and lives in a test tube.
Bozo the Clone.

Minnesota- Folwell Hall

What goes in dry, pink and hard, and comes out wet, pink and soft.

Bubble gum.

Minnesota-Chemical Engineering

What's long, hard and has semen in it?

No, a submarine.

Wisconsin-Spudnut Restaurant

-Polish firing squad

Minnesota-Aeronautic Engineering

-ferrous wheel

Purdue-Library

Defend your right to bear arms!

Ohio State-Thompson Library

. . . and he says, "What's a Hemingway?"

. . . and she says, "Oh, about 6½ pounds."

Iowa-Art

Egg #1: Did you order any furniture?

Egg #2: No, why?

Egg #1: Because two nuts are trying to push an organ up here.

Purdue-Chemistry

Schlock: Did you sleep with my wife last night?

Schmuck: Not a wink.

Michigan-East Engineering

1st cannibal: Are you enjoying your meal?

2nd cannibal: Having a ball.

Wisconsin-Chemical Engineering

Beethoven had a noted career.

Illinois-Physics

Tolkien is hobbit-forming.

Ohio State-Thompson Library

"Lord of the Rings" is a Tolkien effort.

Iowa-Zoology

Mickey Mouse divorced Minnie; she was fuckin' goofey.

Minnesota-Vincent Hall

Mickey Mouse is a rat!

Ohio State-Thompson Library

Walt Disney led an animated life
-below-
Sometimes he was rather goofey.
-below-
No need to Mickey Mouse — he hung around with fairies.

Michigan State-Human Ecology

Lassie is a bitch!

Ohio State-Thompson Library

Jimmy Hoffa — please call home.

Michigan State-Human Ecology

Polanski's new movie - "Close Encounters With The Third Grade."

Iowa-Zoology

Californians are not without faults.

Illinois-Lincoln Hall

Spirochete add a new twist.

Indiana-Myers Hall

Amoeba don't know their heads from their asses.

Wisconsin-White Library

Nostalgia ain't what it used to be.

Michigan-Little Science Building

Who gives a damn about apathy? Not me!

Wisconsin-Social Science

Is dogma the mother of all dogs?

Wisconsin-Humanities

Individualists unite!

Wisconsin-Memorial Library

Organize spontaneity!

Northwestern-Speech

Smash entropy!

Wisconsin-Psychology

There's no future in astrology!

Illinois-Physics

Xerox never does anything original.

Wisconsin-Education

Help! The paranoids are after me.

Indiana-Fine Arts

I'd give my right arm to be ambidextrous.

Indiana-Sycamore Hall

How about the 98-pound weakling who went to Alaska and came back a huskie fucker.

Minnesota-Walter Library

Whoever took a shit, please return it and no questions will be asked.

Ohio State-Dulles Hall

Linda Lovelace's mother died going down on the Titanic.

Iowa-Art

What do you call a member of a Russian motorcycle gang? A Red riding hood.

Iowa-Pharmacy

I hear the Pope is going to tear down the Vatican and put up a pole building.

Iowa-Phillips Hall

God is love.
Love is blind.
Ray Charles is blind.
Therefore . . .

Classic on all campuses

You can kiss a nun once, but don't get in the habit.

Michigan State-Engineering

I'd rather have a bottle in front of me than a frontal lobotomy.

Classic on all campuses

Descartes before the horse.

Wisconsin-Humanities

Eve wore a fig leaf, and Adam wore a hole in it.

Illinois-Undergraduate Library

If you took all the students that sleep in class and laid
them end to end, they'd be a lot more comfortable.

Purdue-Library

At first my wife didn't want to have children, but now she
is having fecund thoughts.

Minnesota-Zoology

Kids who eat breakfast are generally more alert, as well as
being more likely to throw up in gym class.

Michigan-Hatcher Library

This ain't no police station, but a lot of dicks hang out
here.

Minnesota-Zoology

There's only one thing the government can't tax and that's
your peter. Ninety percent of the time it's out of work and just
hanging around, and even when it is working it's in the hole.
Besides, it has two dependents and they're both nuts.

Minnesota-Engineering

I was here. Where were you? Be back soon.

Godot.

Classic on all campuses

I burn my candle at both ends,
and it may not last the night.
But, oh my foes, and oh my friends,
it gives a lovely light.

Edna St. Vincent Millay was here with Kilroy.

Wisconsin-Social Science

Fred is dead.
Ethel

Indiana-Swain Hall

It was a good life, relatively speaking.

Albert Einstein

Illinois-Fine Arts

Reach out, reach out and touch someone.

Ma Bell

(over urinals in mens room)
Minnesota-Zoology

Descarte: To do is to be.
Nietshe: To be is to do.
Sinatra: To be doo be do.

Michigan-Business Administration

Let them eat frozen cake.
                    Charles Birdseye
                              Northwestern-Kresge Hall

Drugs — the next best thing to being there.
                    Alexander Bell
                              Iowa-English/Philosophy

College is a pop quiz; Life is the final.

Minnesota-Chemical Engineering

Some thought is given to the meaning of Life.

Life isn't all it's cracked up to be.

Indiana-Myers Hall

Life is like an enema — you get out of it what you put in plus a lot of shit.

Minnesota-Elliott Hall

Life is like a penis — once you realize you have it you
have to figure out what to do with it.

Wisconsin-425 Henry Mall

Life is a shit sandwich and every day is another bite.

Michigan State-Chemistry

Life is like a shit sandwich; the more bread you have the
less shit you eat.

Illinois-Library

Life is a banquet and most poor bastards are starving.

Ohio State-Thompson Library

Life is like a penis — when it's soft you can't beat it,
but when it's hard you get fucked.

Classic on all campuses

Life as we know it does not exist.

Wisconsin-Humanities

Life brings on watering of the eyes.

Wisconsin-425 Henry Mall

Life would be more simple if I could just settle for being a bum.

Indiana-Swain Hall

Cheer up — you only live once.

Indiana-Myers Hall

For those of you who think Life's a joke, consider the punch line.

Classic on all campuses

Life is its own punchline.

Northwestern-Fisk Hall

Life goes on.

-below-

With its culmination in ever-approaching Death.

Michigan-Hatcher Library

Your lives are graffiti on the walls of Time.

Illinois-Library

The saddest thing in life is to see it as it is rather than as it should be.

Ohio State-Thompson Library

Tell me something good about Life.

        -below-

You can see to read this.

        Illinois-Lincoln Hall

Life resembles the heavens at midnight — basically black and uninviting, although dotted with little twinkling lights. Sometimes Life is obscurred by clouds and the few bright spots present aren't even visible. Now, if we could only predict when it will be cloudy.

        Ohio State-Thompson Library

Today's graffitiists are tomorrow's sages.

Wisconsin-South Hall

Miscellaneous words of wisdom are to be found in Big Ten graffiti.

Violence completes the partial mind.

Purdue-Library

Hatred is an ulcer on the body of brotherhood.

Iowa-Library

Violence is the last refuge of the incompetent.

Wisconsin-White Hall

In order to be, never try to seem.

Michigan State-Engineering

Leave your mark not on the desktop, but in the hearts of those who knew you well.

Purdue-Library

Peace does not dwell in outward things, but within the soul.

Ohio State-Thompson Library

Live for yourself and you will live in vain.
Live for others and you will live again.

Michigan-Hatcher Library

Everyone's pink on the inside.

Minnesota-Aeronautic Engineering

Ugliness is intangible.

Purdue-Library

What's the difference between ignorance and apathy?
I don't know and I don't care.

Wisconsin-Spudnut Restaurant

Don't treat your mind like a savings account.

Wisconsin-YMCA

The key to being an expert is to complicate the simple.

Michigan-Education

Opinions are like assholes — everyone has one and they are usually full of shit.

Minnesota-Smith Hall

Must we find a solution? Can't we just enjoy the problem for awhile?

Wisconsin-Chemical Engineering

Smart people have no reason to live.

Wisconsin-Humanities

As occasional suicide assures the rest of us that the grass is not always greener.

Iowa-Phillips Hall

Time is Nature's way of making sure everything happens at once.

Wisconsin-Social Science

Words mean nothing when Time ends.

Illinois-Library

Ain't no free lunch in this vale of tears.

Ohio State-Union

Realization of one's own mortality would humble even the most arrogant among us.

-below-

It can inspire him to the ultimate arrogance — the attempt to conquer Death itself. In no other endeavor is Man more arrogant or more noble or more right.

Indiana-Swain Hall

You only go around once, but if you work it right once is enough.

Iowa-Library

The only cure for Life and Death is to enjoy the interval in between.

Michigan-Hatcher Library

Man was born to live, not to prepare for Life.

Michigan State-Agriculture

Let's grease up the machinery of Life.

Northwestern-Fisk Hall

Fly high, my little guy.
You'll find the answer by and by.

Michigan-Hatcher Library

Dare to struggle, dare to win.

Michigan-Hatcher Library

What you set out to do will someday come to pass.
All things hang like a drop of dew upon a blade of grass.

Michigan-Hatcher Library

Why is it that the ones who work the hardest never mention
how hard they've worked, whereas those who work little are always
wont to tell it?

Michigan-Hatcher Library

Money is the root of all wealth.

Minnesota-Zoology

Remember the Golden Rule: Those with the gold rule.

Illinois-Burrill Hall

Did you notice that even when you get ahead in the rat race you still feel like a rat.

Classic on all campuses

If there's no free lunch, I'll settle for breakfast.

Wisconsin-Spudnut Restaurant

There's no such thing as a freed man.
Milton Lunch.

Minnesota-Vincent Hall

I complained because I had no shoes until I met a man with no credit cards.

Purdue-Library

Disco is to music what Etch-A-Sketch is to art.

Wisconsin-Humanities

Where does that noisy disco shit come from?
-below-
It bobs to the surface and occasionally turns belly up.

Wisconsin-Spudnut Restaurant

As the dog returns to his vomit, so does the fool return to his folly.

Michigan-Library

If your plans are for one year, plant rice.
If your plans are for five years, plant trees.
If your plans are for a thousand years, educate.

Minnesota-Vincent Hall

Only the most foolish of mice would hide in a cat's ear.
But only the wisest of cats would think to look there.

Minnesota-Tate Laboratory

Only fake people wear real furs.

Indiana-Morrison Hall

Corporations don't have to breed, we do.

Indiana-Morrison Hall

The only serious question is whether or not to commit suicide.

Indiana-Sycamore Hall

A poor alternative can be made to look good when compared
to a worse alternative.

Purdue-Library

The harbor where freedom lies at anchor has not yet been
charted.

Wisconsin-Spudnut Restaurant

Remember, he who made kittens put snakes in the grass.

Ohio State-Lord Hall

Evolution is a lie!

Ohio State-Thompson Library

Change is the essential process of all existence.

Michigan State-Erickson Hall

How many rats ever got cancer from too much pornography?

Illinois-Gregory Hall

Angels can fly because they take themselves lightly.

Purdue-Library

Hi there, you silly savages,

Iowa-Physics

We could find a reason for most of the writings of the Big Ten students. But for some of the graffiti we couldn't even find an excuse. Those pieces are gathered here.

Where does the white go when the snow melts?

Minnesota-Tate Laboratories

Where does the light go when it goes out?

Michigan State-Engineering

Which is further, to Duluth or by bus?

Minnesota-Smith Hall

Can a blue man sing the whites?

Indiana-Myers Hall

Is there gender after Death?

Minnesota-Vincent Hall

Why is there no ham in hamburger?

Ohio State-Hopkins Hall

Why does ice cream have no bones?

Minnesota-Smith Hall

Can a river stop running?

Illinois-Lincoln Hall

What ya gonna do when the well runs dry?

-below-

Drink river water.

Michigan State-Engineering

I have known rivers!

Minnesota-Smith Hall

Let's talk dirty to the animals.

Michigan-Union

Flying turtles are real, they just don't show up on radar.

Purdue-Library

What's the difference between a duck?

Minnesota-Smith Hall

Does the water ripple when a duck farts?

Minnesota-Vincent Hall

Waves are caused by whale farts.

Iowa-Phillips Hall

A fart in the bathtub is a burt.

Wisconsin-Humanities

Hugglebunnyburgers!

Michigan State-Chemistry

A little bird with a yellow bill
sat upon my window sill.
I coaxed him in with bits of bread,
and then I smashed his fuckin' head.

Minnesota-Walter Library

Eliminate the trade deficit - legalize homegrown carrots.

Wisconsin-Chemistry

I see that Zambezzian barley production is up again.

Wisconsin-Chemistry

Rainfall stimulation is obscene.

Wisconsin-Agronomy

Raise the tariff on lumberjacks from Sweden.

Michigan State-Engineering

How long is an art concept?

Wisconsin-Humanities

Moomin Valley is the place to be.

Michigan-Hatcher Library

Scotland is best! Go plaid!

Michigan-West Engineering

The road to Hell is paved with unbought stuffed dogs.

Wisconsin-White Library

Where, oh where, has my little dog gone?

Indiana-Myers Hall

What have they done with my Raggety Ann?

Iowa-Physics

Does your mother know you masturbate?

Ohio State-Thompson Library

Turn back!

      -below-

It's too late!

Ohio State-Thompson Library

The man who laughs last has not been told the terrible truth.

Wisconsin-Humanities

I am beyond good and evil!

Northwestern-Kresge Hall

Time sneaked up and caught me.

Minnesota-Chemical Engineering

I've paid the price of solitude, but at least I'm out of debt.

Michigan State-Library

"I'm not a bad person, I'm a good person. I'm just a bad, bad wizard," Franklin said as he raised the gun to his temple.

Michigan-Haven Hall

Even in pain there is that which is festive.

Wisconsin-Humanities

Suicide feels good when you stop.

Indiana-Memorial Hall

I'm hovering like a fly, waiting for the windshield on a freeway.

Michigan-Hatcher Library

Man is biodegradeable, but contains phosphorous.

Michigan State-Library

Are you one of the famous?

Iowa-Art

Please adjust my vertical hold.

Illinois-Fine Art

Give me 40 acres and I'll turn this rig around.

Indiana-Memorial Hall

It takes a lot to laugh. It takes a train to cry.

Purdue-Library

Better latent than never.

Iowa-Engineering

The train sounds naked.

Iowa-Library

- Mercedes Benzene

Purdue-Heavilon Hall

Viva, Wilbur!
>   *-below-*

In next week's episode Wilbur meets the Pope.
>   *-below-*

What does Wilbur say to the Pope?
>   *-below-*

The Pope smokes dope.
>   *Wisconsin-Social Science*

pi = 3.141492653589793238462
>   *(not checked for accuracy)*
>   *Purdue-Library*

Poor Santa! (he's dead, you know)
>   *Wisconsin-Humanities*

I'm a forester, and that's okay,
I sleep all night and I work all day.
>   *Minnesota-Aeronautic Engineering*

Everyone says, "Give him the soap! Give him the soap!" But soap causes a dangerous film in the tub. I say, "Hold the soap! Hold the soap!"
>   *Wisconsin-YMCA*

If I'm not here, I've gone dancing.
>   *Minnesota-Wilson Library*

No matter how insignificant the experience, we learn.

Northwestern-Technical Institute

We found a great deal to be learned from the graffiti of the Big Ten students. We also found a great deal to be learned from the process of collecting it. Here is some of a great deal.

Graffiti is not limited to any field of study. The pure scientists write graffiti in the stalls of the restrooms. The social scientists do not confine their graffiti to the stalls. They write on the restroom walls, window sills, doors and dispensers. The students of the fine arts do not confine their graffiti at all. It can be found on anything that stands still long enough to be inked. This includes restrooms, classrooms, hallways, windows, doors, ceilings, lockers and any fellow student found in an immobile status.

Graffiti is less abundant in modern buildings of glass and tile, and more abundant in buildings with seasoned wood and flaking paint.

Graffiti is less abundant in adminstrative office buildings than in buildings of large undergraduate classrooms.

Custodians vary in their approach to graffiti. Some take no action. Others are selective, removing that graffiti that they find most offensive. Still others are compulsive removers. The traces of these expungers are commonplace — cleanser rubbings, steelwool scratches, black paint and other more exotic chemicals. The battle between the custodian and student is ongoing.

Some questions came up during our research:

Why do all grad students carry coffee cups and keys?

Where did Michigan get its "Ivy League" student union?

Why are there separate staff restrooms at Illinois?

Why do men write six times as much graffiti as women?

Where do Illinois, Indiana and Michigan get their money?

Why are most of the crazies at Wisconsin?

With this listing of significant questions, we pass the torch to a new generation of scholarly searchers. We trust that our efforts will help light the way toward a greater understanding of cultures other than our own. We wish you good luck and Godspeed.

Beam us up, Scottie!